# The Pixie Chronicles
# The Cat Next Door

**Written and Illustrated by:**
**Riley Sims**

To my mom,

Who heard the story first and helped me edit it and to my cat Pixie
who inspired me.

# Table of Contents

This is the story of Pixie. The cat next door. She eats, sleeps and lies around. But this week, is a different kind of a week.

# CHAPTER I: MONDAY
## Cats and More Cats

Pixie is on her porch, when all of a sudden there are flinging claws coming right at her! She doesn't know who is attacking her. Then a thought comes to her. It's probably *him*!

Sorry to interrupt, but Pixie's sworn enemy is Boots, the most annoying cat on the block.

Back to the story. Pixie looks fiercely at Boots.

"Boots what are you doing? I'm too lazy to fight" she says.

"I guess I win this one!" Boots responds with a sneer.

As Boots turns around to go back, Pixie throws her short claws into Boots' behind. Boots meows.

"That's what you get for disturbing my nap!

Boots decides he is going to fight back, but suddenly a cat appears from the open door. It's Nyla! Pixie's best friend.

Nyla gives a stern look over in Boots' direction. Her eyes are glaring and she looks like she is about to give Boots another scratch on the behind.

"What did I tell you about bothering Pixie?!"

Boots starts to run, but Nyla catches up to him.

"Answer me!" she meows.

"Yeah… I remember" Boots answers visibly shaken.

"Then explain yourself!" Nyla insists.

Boots looks terrified.

"Well, I umm… got to run!"

Boots runs away. Nyla goes back to check on Pixie.

"Pixie, are you ok? Are you hurt?"

Nyla always was like a mother to Pixie even though she is only a year older.

"Yeah, yeah I'm fine." Pixie says looking bothered.

"Well, anyway, I am glad you are ok. It's dinner time and we should go inside."

The two can always count on each other in good times and bad.

# CHAPTER II: TUESDAY
## Apples and Bananas

Pixie doesn't know what to do today, but Nyla suggests making an apple and banana pie.

"That sounds like a great idea Nyla!"

The two get to work. First, they get some apples and bananas. They use their paws to mash it all up.

"Let's get a bowl" says Pixie, realizing that all of the food is on the table.

Nyla sets up a bowl, throwing all the fruit inside. They continue mashing with their paws until Pixie grabs a jar with sugar.

"How much sugar do we need in this?" asks Nyla.

"I think it's as much as we want!" Pixie answers purring.

Nyla encouragingly proceeds to throw in several pawfulls of grainy, white sugar. Pixie tastes the batter. She immediately spits it out.

"This is gross!" she cries. "It has no salt in it. It needs salt!"

Nyla carefully listens and adds a few pawfulls of salt. Pixie tastes again.

"Ewwww! This is too much salt! It needs more sugar!"

Nyla adds some more sugar again, throwing a distrustful look over at Pixie. Pixie starts to get visibly upset, since the pie isn't coming together the way she thought it would.

"Let's try again" she says.

The two work together, this time adding both sugar and salt sparingly.

Success! The pie is finished and smells delicious. Suddenly, Boots pops up from the window. He jumps and grabs the pie right off the counter.

"Catch him!" meows Nyla, running after Boots.

"It's too late Nyla, it's too late!" cries Pixie.

"But we have to catch him!" Nyla bellows.

"Or… we could just make some cupcakes instead!" suggests Pixie.

"Alright, we can do that I guess" Nyla agrees hesitantly.

The two set off to make cupcakes, while Boots happily enjoys his pie out on the street.

# CHAPTER III: WEDNESDAY
## Cyberius the Dog

Pixie is wondering around the neighborhood, until she comes up to 482 Milview Drive. She is terrified at the thought of who lives there, because it happens to be a big dog named Cyberius. Pixie knows that he rules the neighborhood. She tries to walk past his house calmly, but suddenly hears a low growling noise. It's Cyberius! Pixie is just about to run away, but Cyberius crosses her path.

"And where do you think you are going little kitty?" Cyberius asks.

"I was just going home after circling the neighborhood" answers Pixie in a very low and shaking voice.

"Well, guess what?! You are not allowed on this turf, because this is my territory." Cyberius barks.

Pixie attempts to run home once more. This time she succeeds.

"That's what I thought little kitty" Cyberius cries while chasing after Pixie, forcing her to run even faster. "Run along while you still can!"

Pixie is petrified at the thought that she might die. She meows for Nyla, but Nyla is nowhere to be seen.

"Nyla!" she cries suddenly coming to a stop.

Cyberius appears from behind her now, grinning, with Nyla in between his teeth.

"Looking for this?" he exclaims holding Nyla by the collar.

"Nyla!" Pixie meows scared.

But Nyla is knocked out and unresponsive. Cyberius knows that Nyla is a master of Tae Kwon Do and was prepared to fight her.

Pixie is in shock.

"How did youuu..? Hooooow?" she trails off as her sentences get caught in her throat.

Cyberius tosses Nyla towards Pixie.

"This is no use. I am going to take a nap" he says in an abrupt, tired voice.

He waddles back home, knowing that his owner will be mad at him for leaving the house unsupervised.

Nyla wakes up a few minutes later with a pounding headache. She realized that she is very hungry.

"I just need something to eat! It's been a day!" she proclaims. (It's been ten minutes since her last meal.)

The two go home together, walking themselves down the street. Pixie is grateful that Cyberius gave up, because today has been a

looooong day and she just wants to stretch out and relax. Nyla too
is grateful that she is able to go home to a nice meal.

# CHAPTER IV: THURSDAY
## The Higbie Race

Every year there is a big race. Cyberius always has the advantage of winning, since his house is at the end of block where the race ends. Pixie is feeling down, since there is no way she or anyone else can win this race given Cyberius' obvious advantage. But this year, Pixie is chosen to be the race leader and as the leader, she can choose where the race ends. So, after thinking about it some, she chooses Nyla's house to be the official end of the race.

The race begins.

-   "On your marks, get set, go!" the judge cries.

Everyone starts to race to Nyla's house. Pixie and Nyla get a little scared in the beginning with all the commotion. They start to run together. A second later, Cyberius pushes them aside with his long legs and threatening muzzle. Nyla and Pixie aren't sure if they are going to be able to win, but continue running.

"C'mon Nyla, let's go!" Pixie encourages.

"Ugh" mutters Nyla, "I don't want to be running right now."

"Nyla, don't be such a lazy cat" Pixie snorts.

"Fine, let's just get it over with."

"Let's see if we can slow down Cyberius by digging our claws into his back" Pixie yells as she increases her speed.

"Yippee" responds Nyla, excited about the possibility of bringing down Cyberius.

Nyla is so happy that she begins to overtake Pixie and catches up with Cyberius rather quickly.

"Wait, up!" Pixie cries after her.

"We've got no time to lose" Nyla responds breathless.

Pixie catches up. They race after Cyberius. As they catch up, both dig their claws into his back. Cyberius wails in pain slowing down.

"How did you guys catch up to me?" he barks dismayed.

"No time to lose, we've got a race to win" Nyla and Pixie respond in unison, running ahead, thrilled at the thought that they might win the race for the first time in three years.

The two make it to the finish line together, but to their surprise, Boots is laying down on the hot cement, waving his tale from side to side and purring happily. He knows he beat out everyone.

"How did you win?" Pixie asks, feeling a bit disappointed that her win against Cyberius meant nothing.

"Oooh, just the old, jolly flap jack trick" Boots responds with a sly grin.

"But that's banned!" Nyla cries outraged, knowing perfectly well the trick involves cutting corners and making other contestants trip.

"Too bad, so sad" Boots exclaims marching towards his shiny, new trophy. "I like winning! Feels great!"

"But that's unfair!" Pixie meows.

"Life is unfair," Boots shouts, running off with his prize.

Nyla and Pixie walk home together once again. They may not have won today, but they always have their friendship.

# CHAPTER V: FRIDAY
## Weekend Eve

It is weekend eve, the best time of the week. Everyone gets excited about it, as the next few days are all about relaxation. Pixie is hyped. She is so excited that she rushes over to Nyla's house faster than a bolt. Nyla is in the process of cleaning herself off when Pixie barges in.

"Pixie, what are you doing here?"

"Well, I thought I would drop by for a visit since it is almost the weekend and I don't have anything to do."

"Oh yes! It is almost the weekend!" cries Nyla. "Tonight, there will be fireworks I hear."

"That sounds so fun. Can we go?"

"Pixie, you don't have to ask me twice."

"Alright, let's go!" meows Pixie.

"But your hair is unbrushed" replies Nyla.

The two take the time to get themselves ready for the fireworks spectacular. Pixie and Nyla do a good job of preparing and at nine p.m. sharp set off to watch the fireworks.

They arrive at the waterfront, noticing that many have come to watch.

"I am sorry everyone, but fireworks are canceled today due to heavy fog" a booming voice announces into the microphone from nearby.

"What?!" Pixie cries. "What are we going to do now Nyla?"

"Sorry Pixie, I guess we are not going to see any fireworks tonight" responds Nyla disappointed.

"Do you think that we might be able to watch a movie that has fireworks in it instead?" asks Pixie.

"That's a good idea!" announces Nyla somewhat cheered up.

The two start to head home to watch their movie together, but suddenly Boots appears out of the bushes.

"Can I join you guys for the evening?" he meows sadly.

"Umm, alright" the two agree hesitantly, while exchanging confused looks. They are not sure they can trust Boots, but he seems genuinely lonely.

The three then walk together silently, until noticing a fourth shadow in an alleyway. They pick up their speed to avoid trouble.

"Not so fast!" says Cyberius coming out of the dark, his eyes fixed directly on the three standing by the soft light of the street lamp.

They want to get away quickly and be able to watch a movie together without any trouble from Cyberius.

"Would any of you be interested in watching fireworks tonight with me? I know a place where we will be able to see them, despite the fog."

Boots, Pixie, and Nyla throw distrusting glances over at Cyberius. Do they take their chances or continue home to watch a movie?

"Let's give it a try" announces Pixie. "But if you even think about pulling anything with us, you will learn to regret it."

"Tonight, I am more interested in watching the fireworks than messing with you three" Cyberius barks back, visibly bothered.

They follow Cyberius to watch the fireworks. Ordinarily, they wouldn't have trusted him, but it is weekend eve and they are looking for something fun to do. Watching real fireworks seems much more exciting than a movie.

They finally make it to the fireworks show. To their mutual surprise, it is a lot of fun! They enjoy themselves and for the first time, trust each other. Perhaps they are not so different after all. In the end, they did have a great time and just maybe, could all become good friends.

# CHAPTER VI: SATURDAY
## Weekend Party

Pixie is chilling at home because it's the weekend and everyone gets a chance to relax. It has always been this way, ever since Pixie was a little kitten. But this weekend, she wants to change it up, so she makes up her mind to have a themed party. She decides the theme of the party will be angels and devils. Pixie is so excited by the thought of hosting her own party that she accidentally breaks the most prized vase in the house.

"Oops," she says to no one in particular. "Whoever asks, it is not my fault," she runs off giggling to Nyla's house.

"Nyla, Nyla, Nyla, Nyla" she meows repeatedly.

"What is it?" Nyla answers still sleepy from her nap.

"I am going to host a party today. Do you want to come?"

"Hmm... let me think about it. Nah, I want to sleep."

"Nyla please, this is my first party."

"Alright, alright. I'll come to your party if it means so much to you."

"Good. Now let's go back to my house and start planning."

"Wait, hold on. I thought I was a guest, not a planner" Nyla responds feeling inconvenienced.

"You are both, since you are my best friend and I need your help with planning."

The two head over to Pixie's house and begin prepping for the party. They work hard all afternoon decorating and making their costumes. They also post fliers all around the neighborhood to advertise tonight's event. Even Cyberius is invited! Pixie dresses up as an angel and suggests that Nyla dress up as a devil so that they can be in sync.

It is soon time for the party and the two are ready to host. All the guests storm in at 7 p.m. sharp, just as the flyer announced. Everyone is here! It is the most exciting event the neighborhood has ever seen and all are dressed for the party. So many angels and devils in one room!

Nyla is surprised by the amazing turnout and loves being a host. Out of the corner of her eye, she notices Cyberius waltz in, looking like the true devil dog that he is at times. Nyla assesses her devil costume to be much better than Cyberius'.

"What do you think of my costume?" Cyberius asks both Nyla and Pixie.

"It looks just like you!" Nyla responds, taking a dig at him.

"Hey! I thought since you invited me to this party, we were going to call it a truce for the night?"

"Well, Pixie invited you. My vote is still out" Nyla retorts.

"Wow, I thought you might be an angel for a second," Cyberius compliments Pixie trying hard to ignore Nyla at this point.

"Thank you! I worked hard at my costume."

A judge comes up to the microphone to announce the winner of the best costume of the night.

"And the winner is…. PIXIE!"

Pixie gasps in surprise. The judge makes a comment that Pixie's fur is so white, that she could have really passed for an angel. Pixie is so excited to have finally won something. Everyone is congratulating her when Boots suddenly gets up to the microphone and announces himself to be the winner.

"I am the best dressed in this room! You should all be congratulating me!" he states with a serious tone.

Cyberius takes it upon himself to handle the matter and walks up to Boots growling in his deepest voice imaginable. Boots scrambles off the stage, afraid his practical joke is not received well by the crowd. The judge then quickly tells everyone not to worry and continue to go about their business, once again declaring Pixie as the winner.

Pixie walks up to the stage to make her speech.

"Hello," she begins. "I want to thank everyone for coming to my party tonight and I also want to split this trophy with you all for being such great guests and my friends."

Everyone roars with excitement. Pixie cannot believe her eyes and ears. She loves being able to share her win with so many great friends. The trophy happens to be made almost entirely of Chewy, a cat's best dessert, and Pixie lets everyone take a lick. All her friends get a taste and it is delicious!

The party is a huge success and all leave happy. Pixie and Nyla save some of the trophy for themselves, quietly enjoying the rest of the evening out on the porch together, purring with enjoyment.

# CHAPTER VII: SUNDAY
## A Helping Paw

Pixie is walking along the street when she sees an animal care center. She walks in, but there is no one there to greet her. The place is empty. She sees three cats and one puppy in the corner. She decides to get Nyla to come back together and check on what's going on inside.

"Pixie, why do I have to do everything you do?" Nyla complains.

"Because you are my best friend and that is what best friends do for each other" Pixie explains.

"Well, not this best friend" Nyla turns around to leave.

Suddenly, Nyla hears a feeble bark from the corner of the room. She turns to find a little, white pup who looks up at her pleadingly.

"See, this is why we can't leave. I think this place has been abandoned by its owners and these animals are hungry and alone."

"Ok, ok" Nyla responds, realizing that she might need to stay and help.

"Are you ok little pup?" she asks.

"I don't know. It's been two days since I last ate and am starving" the pup barks back.

"Nyla, let's get everyone here some food!" Pixie declares.

The two head over to the Tuna Canoe, a local pet store in the neighborhood.

"C'mon, let's get some tuna and some dog food," Pixie says pointing at the top shelf where all the cans of food are stacked.

"But Pixie, how are we ever going to reach that shelf? It is really high up" Nyla meows discouraged.

At this very moment the store bell rings and in walks Cyberius.

"What great timing!" Pixie cries. "Can you help us reach that food on the top shelf?"

"Sure. I can get it," Cyberius bends his hind legs in preparation for a jump. He knocks a few cans of tuna as well as some dog food off the top shelf.

"What is this for?" Cyberius asks puzzled, noticing bags of dog food.

"Come see for yourself" Pixie responds, giving Cyberius an encouraging nod to follow them out of the store.

Nyla and Pixie lead Cyberius to the care center.

"Whoa, why am I here?" Cyberius asks confused.

"Look in that corner" Nyla points.

Cyberius gasps at the sight of the little puppy whimpering in the corner.

"What happened here?" he asks concerned.

"These animals were left behind" Nyla and Pixie explain.

"How could someone just leave them all like this?" Cyberius asks looking from corner to corner and noticing all the other animals in distress.

"We don't know, but they could all use our help" Pixie responds.

Suddenly there is chuckling nearby. It's Boots and he is holding a baby kitten in his mouth.

"Boots, what are you doing here?" the three ask in one voice.

"I noticed that no one was running this place a day or so ago, and decided to stop by to check on the animals."

"Why do you think someone would just leave them all here like this Boots?" Cyberius asks.

"I think the owners had a sudden emergency and had to leave town rather quickly. I am not sure they had time to get someone else in here to take care of this place."

"Well, I guess we will have to step up and take care of the center while the owners are away" Pixie suggests. "I know we don't all get along, but this can be a perfect opportunity to come together and do something important for the neighborhood."

"I guess we can give it a shot" Boots agrees hesitantly.

The three work together for the next few hours to distribute the food around the center, making sure each animal gets their share. Soon enough, everyone is fed and happy and Pixie, Nyla, Cyberius and Boots realize that they can work together for the good of the neighborhood and put their differences aside.

They each go home happy that day, knowing that they had done something important for someone in need. Pixie and Nyla will always be best friends, but it is nice to know that they can rely on Cyberius and Boots to lend a paw when needed.

It has been a long week for Pixie. Certainly, a different kind of a week. She is looking forward to her rest and can now go back to eating, sleeping and lying around.

# ABOUT THE AUTHOR

Riley Dae Sims is a nine-year-old girl with a great imagination. She loves to read and express herself through writing and drawing. She has loved stories for as long as she can remember. Although she's penned a few that have not been published, 'The Pixie Chronicles' is her very first full-length book. She hopes to write many more. Her passions include building Legos, playing flute, singing and performing. She plans to combine writing and acting someday.